the little book of
CRYSTALS

Published by OH!
20 Mortimer Street
London W1T 3JW

Disclaimer:

ISBN 978-1-91161-061-8

Editorial: Victoria Godden
Project manager: Russell Porter
Design: Ben Ruocco
Production: Rachel Burgess

A CIP catalogue record for this book is available from the British Library

Printed in China

10 9 8 7 6

the little book of
CRYSTALS

beleta greenaway

CONTENTS

Introduction   6

Chapter 1
Buying, preparing and
storing crystals   8

Chapter 2
Crystal descriptions   22

Chapter 3
All about crystals   78

Chapter 4
Crystal chakra colours   102

Chapter 5
Crystals and magic   112

Chapter 6
Crystals and nature   168

Chapter 7
Crystals for ailments   176

Conclusion   189
Index   190

INTRODUCTION

Crystals form in nature when liquids cool and start to harden, and certain molecules in the liquid gather as they attempt to become stable. They do this in a repeating pattern. In our natural surroundings, they can be made when liquid rock that is called magma cools, but some can be formed in an element named carbon. At school, many of us were shown how to grow crystals in a short time frame, but other stones can take many thousands of years to form and develop. For example, diamonds are a crystal form of carbon, caused by high temperatures and high pressure, and they were created when the Earth was young.

Diamonds are thought to take between one and three billion years to grow, but the oldest crystal found on Earth is a zircon which is believed to be 3.3 billion years old. Considering the Earth is thought to be 4.345 billion years old, it is clear that these crystals were fashioned from the early days of our planet's history. The influences around the formation of crystals can have a dramatic effect. Graphite and diamonds are both carbon-based crystals: one produces pencil lead, the other, a valuable jewel. Some are like diamonds, very durable; others are not.

Salt is a crystal that dissolves in water, and as a rough guide, crystals names ending in 'ite' are also often water-soluble. They are formed in seven shapes – cubic, hexagonal, monoclinic, orthorhombic, tetragonal, triclinic and trigonal. It is probable that the most well-known crystal shape is the snowflake, where the ice flake shape radiates out in a regulated flower shape. There are so many types and varieties of crystals across the globe that is it impossible to list them all, but in this little book we will embark upon a journey to discover the more common stones and explore some of their uses today.

CHAPTER

1

BUYING, PREPARING
and
STORING CRYSTALS

It is always best to purchase crystals from a store rather than online.

This is because the crystal often "chooses" its owner. Find a good crystal shop and spend at least an hour in the store. The chances are that the sales assistant will have a vast knowledge of crystal properties and he or she will help you select the right ones.

Don't choose
with your
EYES

People are often drawn to the pretty crystals that shout out "pick me", but often it is the less attractive or asymmetrical stones that hold the greatest power. Place one crystal in each hand and concentrate on the stones. One hand might tingle, it might feel hot or cold, or it could even begin to ache. If there are any such sensations, it is likely that the crystal has chosen you.

CARING
for
CRYSTALS

Crystals absorb energy from individuals and from places, and they act like a sponge. Throughout a crystal's life, it will have been touched and handled by a lot of people, so before a crystal can be used it must be cleansed and energised thoroughly to rid it of any vibrations that it may have soaked up along the way.

salt
CLEANSING

Salt is a purifier that will cleanse the stone of any impurities, leaving it spiritually disinfected. Pour a large amount of any kind of salt, such as household salt or sea salt, in a bowl and bury the crystal in it for twenty-four hours.

RAINWATER
cleansing

Rainwater possesses powerful cleansing properties, and for some crystals is a good way to free the stone of any vibrational contaminations. On a rainy day, collect some rainwater in a bowl and soak the crystal in the liquid for a few hours. Do check to make sure the crystal is nonporous first, as some crystals might fall apart if soaked.

SUN and MOON
cleansing

Placing crystals outside overnight to bathe in the moon's rays is an excellent way to purify your stone. Many believe that the full moon and the new moon are the best phases for crystal cleansing. Leaving them outside on a sunny day is also favourable, but do check to see that your stone isn't one of those that might fade in sunlight. Some of the quartz stones should be kept out of the sun.

SAGE
cleansing

Another quick and simple way to cleanse your crystal's energy is to use sage. Light some sage incense or use a white sage smudging stick and hold the crystal in your hand, allowing the crystal to drift in and out of the smoke. After a few minutes, place the crystal beside the incense stick or rest the smudging stick in a bowl, and when the burning comes to an end, your crystal will be bathed.

ENERGISING
crystals

Bad weather is believed to energise crystals, making them more powerful in general. If a person wants to obtain high-impact energy from their crystal, they should wait for a thunder and lightning storm and place the crystal outside on a window ledge. Blustery days, hailstorms and strong winds are also thought to enhance the power of crystals.

CHARGING
crystals

An easy way to charge a crystal is to hold it in your hand and imagine white light coming down from the universe and flooding the crystal with power. While this is going on, ask that the crystal should be used for the highest good. Alternatively, hold the crystal in some incense smoke.

crystal GROUPS

When a person has a selection of different kinds of crystals, it is always best to research which crystals respond well to others. If a person places a lot of stones all in one place, their energies can become distorted. For instance, some people find when visiting crystal shops that they feel a surge of energy when they walk through the door, and some people even experience a headache. If your crystals have become jumbled with other crystals or left out to gather unwanted energies, cleanse and charge them again.

STORING
crystals

Those who use crystals for healing purposes might not want to leave their stones out on display where they can absorb unwanted energy, which will reduce their ability to work properly. Crystals shouldn't be allowed to soak up the vibrations of their environment. Cover these stones in a clean cloth or scarf and house them in a drawer.

CHAPTER

2

CRYSTAL DESCRIPTIONS

This chapter lists a number of crystals, some of which are well known and others obscure. I will describe the appearance of the crystals and show how they can be used. You will see several of these crystals scattered throughout this book, along with many others in the chapters offering guidance on crystal uses for solving practical problems, emotional problems, magical purposes, for healing, helping others and more. The size of this book precludes listing full details of all the stones.

AGATE

Agate comes in a variety of colours that are in bands, with blue and brown being the most common. When a person has undergone great stress and is in an emotional state, this crystal can soothe their temper.

It is also said to improve the digestive system, hiatus hernias and concentration.

AMETHYST

This beautiful lavender-coloured quartz has been used for jewellery throughout the ages and it is known as a healing crystal. Children especially respond to it, as it calms and soothes their nervous systems.

If you find yourself living in a disruptive house, amethyst quietens down anger and violence. This is a brilliant healing stone to hold when meditating and it is great to use as a pendulum for divination.

AMBLYGONITE

This delicate white, pale lemon or green crystal can unleash the artistic side of a person and inspire them to be creatively individual and inventive. If there is a potential for the person to be psychic or spiritual, amblygonite can unlock any psychic blocks and bring a clearer understanding of all things mystical.

BARIM

or baryte

This vivid, amber mineral crystallises to form tabular crystals and occasionally stalactites. When placed on the crown chakra or the third eye (the brow chakra), it is said to awaken the Kundalini, thus raising the vibration of the person so they are able to connect to spiritual guides or grand masters. This is a great crystal to use for astral projection.

BERYL

Beryl is a crystal that comes in a variety
of colours. In the past this semi-precious
stone was made into crystal balls for
scrying. It is still highly valued by modern
witches, and often a piece of beryl will
be fitted to the end of the witch's wand.
It has a therapeutic energy for removing
negativity.

CACOXENITE

Cacoxenite is a good vibrational-raising crystal, as it can help other crystals that might need energising. Its colours blend from purple to brown and yellow. Traditionally it represents riches, success, royalty, power and enthusiasm. It is said to release negative energy, thus purifying the soul and spirit and enabling it to enter a new phase.

CASSITERITE

Cassiterite is a black shiny mineral which has integrated shades of beige, pale coral and lemon. This wonderful crystal can help an individual to connect with the higher self and it gives strength and protection when the person is being criticised, bullied and treated unfairly, especially in the workplace. It is said to protect against racial tension or colour prejudice.

CARNELIAN

Carnelian comes in colours of brownish red, red and orange, and it is thought to help with childbirth. It certainly calms down any unhappy emotions, yet despite its calming attributes, it is also an energising crystal, because if placed beside other crystals or inside geodes, it will give the other stones a powerful charge. This stone also helps to heal lethargy and gives a person inner strength.

CITRINE

Citrine is a stone believed to hold the power of the sun, with its shimmering yellow shades. Other colours include deeper oranges and even dark brown. Citrine removes obstacles and blockages from life and it is believed to bring peace to warring families. It is a useful aid to those who need an injection of money as it can bring abundance. If worn, it will help a woman who is suffering from menopausal symptoms and can also bring relief from menstrual cramps.

DATOLITE

Datolite contains hues of pale green and off-white, but also comes in many other shades. If a person has troublesome neighbours, this crystal will calm situations down and lessen anxiety. Placed on the third eye chakra (the brow chakra), it aids psychic vision. Datolite is a great problem-solver and can help to uncover hidden mysteries.

DIAMOND

Diamonds are a girl's best friend!
Diamonds are said to have twenty-
seven different colours, with pale
yellow being especially pretty.
The crystal promotes vitality and
passion, which helps to make
it the most favoured stone for
engagement rings or eternity rings.

EMERALD

The emerald is usually a vivid green but has a range of other hues too. Emerald is associated with friendship and romantic bliss and is said to bring domestic happiness. It is a very sensitive crystal that links to empathy and healing, and it will inspire others to make a new start with confidence. It is linked to the heart chakra and, thus, to unconditional love. It is a truly inspiring gemstone.

ERYTHRITE

(cobalt boom)

Erythrite has a deep magenta to pink colour, and most of these crystals are formed in clusters. This is a beautiful crystal to display in the home, and apart from looking good, it brings a positive healing energy. This crystal is purported to give confidence and articulation when giving a speech, or when teaching or training and giving inspiration to others.

FLUORITE

Fluorite comes in delicate shades of lavender and green. For crystal lovers, fluorite is a must for their collection. It can be used against psychic attack, especially during sleep, and it will keep negative people out of one's orbit. When moving into a new home, it can act as a good energy healer, removing the previous owners' negative vibrations.

FUCHSITE

This gorgeous crystal comes in a variety of turquoise and green shades, and in spiritual circles it is well known as the healing stone. If dramatic changes are needed in a person's life, such as a new home, a love interest or a job opportunity, this mineral can attract positive energy to them and it can be life-changing and very beneficial.

GABBRO

Gabbro is a black speckled volcanic stone from Madagascar, and it is purported to guard against lung and heart disorders. Also, if an individual is feeling out of sorts and needs some energy, this powerful crystal can help. It is a great stone to use for healing and also for those who wish to astral travel to the spiritual realms, or to discover information about Earth's destiny and mankind's future.

GOLDSTONE

Goldstone promotes self-confidence, especially if a person has to go for an interview, or give a presentation or a speech. This crystal of power will inspire motivation and it will see off any negative competition. The colours of the stone are burnt orange with gold dots that make it fascinating to look at. Gaze at this crystal for meditation, successful work and good exam results.

HEMATITE

Hematite is a multipurpose stone which is known to be helpful for those lacking courage and confidence. It can make a woman cope better if she has a bullying man in her life and it can calm down disruptive children. Placing a hematite crystal under a pillow can balance irregular sleep patterns. Its colours are black or dark grey and it usually has a shiny appearance.

HEMIMORPHITE

This stunning crystal has hues of pale teal to the more unusual shades of pale lemon, and when it is heated, it emits an electrical charge. Many spiritual people who wish to enter the angelic realms in dream sleep will use this stone to meditate, with a hope of ascending into a different vibration or visiting the astral plane.

IOLITE

This attractive crystal comes in amazing hues of blue, which can also be shot through with gold dashes. The tumbled stones or cabochons (rounded shapes rather than sharply faceted ones) are much darker but still as powerful. If a person is on a spiritual pathway, this can aid astral travel and keep them safe when out of the body. Iolite is useful for meditation, healing and soul journeying.

IRONSTONE

This mineral has hues of brown and burnt orange and many are banded into attractive stripes. Its main purpose is to banish negative energies and dispel fear of disruptive people. This is a good crystal to use when travelling, or when a person is out of their comfort zone. Backpackers can benefit from carrying a piece of this in their rucksacks.

JADE

Jade has an array of interesting colours that range from purple to lavender, black, blue and green. It is highly prized in China where it is said to bring good luck and abundance. If a female has problems with fertility, this crystal is known to help because it is linked to the reproductive organs. It's a soothing stone that helps to combat insomnia.

JASPER

This attractive mineral comes in a
multitude of different colours; some
of the crystals are banded, dotted and
splashed with interesting patterns.
Jasper is a powerful stone that brings
tranquillity and harmony to anyone
who is lost or disorientated mentally or
physically. Some theorists believe it can
clear electromagnetic pollution.
Pet healers favour jasper to create a
mental connection to animals while
giving them healing.

KINOITE

One of the more psychic crystals, kinoite is often used by mediums and clairvoyants to enhance their spiritual abilities. Its colours are a blue and copper mix, which make it an attractive and interesting crystal. It is said to enhance communication and telepathy. Brides should have a little piece of this pushed into their bouquet for fidelity, peace and love.

KUNZITE

This enchanting crystal comes in amazing shades of violet and rose pink and is eagerly sought when made into jewellery. A rarer colour is the green and yellow blend, and this is known as green kunzite. Because of its purity, it is purported to mend a broken heart or heal the grieving process when one loses a family member.

LABRADORITE

This amazing crystal has fairy-like colours that resemble oil on water, and when gazing into it, the crystal seems to emit feelings of magic and mystery. Many clairvoyants, mediums, healers and therapists will have a piece of this to wear, or they will keep a larger piece of crystal in their homes because it awakens deep psychic abilities and feelings of peace and tranquillity.

LAZULITE

This stunning crystal has mysterious shades of blue and green and looks like something from another planet. When worn as jewellery, it is said to calm a person and give confidence, especially if confrontation is expected and especially in the workplace. Lazulite is used for deep meditation and lucid dreaming, not to mention healing migraines, neck tension and frustrations.

MALACHITE

A vivid teal-coloured crystal which is
swirled or banded in deeper shades.
Malachite is often called the crystal of
transformation and healing. Place a piece
of this mineral in a small cup of rainwater
for a few hours and then bathe tired and
sore eyes with the water. Malachite
orbs are soothing when used as a worry
stone. Be careful not to drink malachite
as it is toxic.

MOLDAVITE

This is one of the most powerful crystals of all, because it is extraterrestrial stone that has become quite rare now. Not a particularly beautiful crystal, it looks like bottle green glass, but it has a tremendous mind-changing impact on individuals. It is often used to increase psychic powers and to unblock any obstacles, but if worn at night it can bring strange dreams.

MOON STONE

Moonstone has an opal-like appearance with pale shades of blue, cream and white. Just like its name, it is associated with the moon and its cycles. When worn it is believed to unlock and assist any psychic abilities the wearer might possess and is often used in meditations to open the mind.

NATROLITE

Natrolite is a clear white tetragonal crystal which has a powerful and positive effect on calming down the nervous system. It seems to have the ability to harmonise whatever may be out of sequence with the body, and to align the chakras to create a healing ambiance. When looking for answers, this stone will help you because it acts like a search engine.

NUUMMITE

Nuummite's appearance is quite unassuming, but don't be fooled by this, as it is a very powerful crystal. When worn as an amulet it can help an individual to discover what's going on in hidden situations and deceptions. One could liken it to a private detective, as it strips away deceit and lies, to bring the truth out into the open.

OBSIDIAN

Black obsidian is a much-loved crystal that is used for many situations; for instance, when a house is haunted, it can protect the owner from psychic attack. Apache tears obsidian offers protection to children when they are sad and frightened. Place a piece of this crystal on their bedside table to help them get a better night's sleep.

OPAL

This is a mysterious gemstone that changes colour in certain lights. It is favoured by spiritual people and is linked to the angelic realms. In folklore, if opals dislike your vibration, they will disappear or the stones will fall out of jewellery, and because of this, they can be deemed unlucky. On the plus side, this is a seductive crystal that will bring passion and love.

PERIDOT

This beautiful lime green gemstone is popular in jewellery and rarely goes out of fashion. It can be used to prevent insomnia and to open the heart to optimism and confidence. Spite and jealousy are the most unpleasant emotions, but peridot can help to disperse them. If a person wants a new relationship, this crystal can help someone to find companionship.

PREHNITE

This pale apple green crystal looks similar to jade and is becoming more popular as a jewellery item. It represents the angel Raphael, as it is a healing stone that evokes unconditional love and connects the individual to the spiritual realms. If the crystal is placed under a pillow it can help a person to focus on dreams and premonitions.

QUARTZ (clear)

Quartz has many uses, and it's especially powerful for energising and amplifying other crystals to bring them back to their former power. Our watches have quartz crystal in them to keep the exact time, and they were also used in the atomic bomb! They are some of the most dynamic healing crystals and many people notice that they can feel their power. It is also a good substitute for any other crystal, so if you don't have the right one to hand for a specific purpose, use a bit of clear quartz instead.

QUARTZ

(faden)

When a relationship is in jeopardy,
with a partner, a child or a friend, this
beautiful clear crystal can build bridges
for harmony and unity. As this is a delicate
stone that absorbs vibrations quickly,
make sure it is fully cleansed in tepid
water and left on a window sill for a few
hours before using it.

RHYOLITE

Rhyolite is an attractive crystal with shades of green, gold and beige. When one is stuck in the past, particularly childhood, this mineral can free the individual and make room for the future to come in, so it gives healing and helps the person to live in the moment. Rhyolite is well known to animal lovers as it promotes understanding and protection for the creatures of the world.

ROSE QUARTZ

This lovely pink stone is extremely popular and many people wear it in a polished form as jewellery. It is linked to love, affection, companionship and good company, so if an individual has been feeling lonely or unloved, charging and using this crystal, and especially wearing a piece of it, can help to unblock the situation and allow friendship and love to come in.

RUBY

Rubies are highly prized for their beauty, but as a true gemstone, they are very expensive. This crystal expresses prosperity and devotion, but also high expectations. It is said that rubies bring joy and laughter. Because of this, many couples will select a ruby for the bride's engagement ring and later eternity ring. It is also well known to endow boldness and a taste for new adventures.

SELENITE

This clear white, opaque crystal is used when people wish to open themselves psychically and spiritually. It is linked to the angelic vibration that helps the person using it to become more centred. It also generates money and good fortune, so gemstone collectors will class selenite as a lucky crystal, and they often give their nearest and dearest a small piece to keep the cash flowing.

SODALITE

A vivid blue crystal, marbled with beige and white shades, this is a good aid to soothing panic attacks. If a piece of this is kept in a person's pocket, especially when out and about, it can prevent a panic attack coming on. When teenagers are lethargic or lazy, this crystal can motivate them to get up and go and to develop a better energy flow.

TANZANITE

This beautiful crystal ranges from deep indigo blue to varying lavender shades and it is becoming very rare because it is only found in Tanzania. Healers who practice Indigo Healing use very esoteric systems such as the seven rays, along with this crystal for meditation and spiritual mastery. The beloved stone is coveted as a betrothal ring for witches during a traditional wedding ceremony known as "handfasting".

TIGER'S EYE

Tiger's eye is a brownish stone with streaks of yellow that is known for its protective qualities. This crystal will prevent any negativity or evil from reaching the owner and it will encourage divine powers to protect the person. Used widely for meditation and for opening the mind to all things spiritual – most importantly, it casts out the evil eye.

TURQUOISE

This blue-green stone is connected to the feminine energies of goddesses and spiritual beings, and it has been valued throughout history as jewellery. In magic circles, it is the most powerful stone of protection and it is often worn as an amulet around the neck to ward off the evil eye. It is said to awaken spiritual energy and communication. Native Americans of the first nation tribes venerate the turquoise crystal.

ULEXITE

This opaque crystal is said to open the third eye (the brow chakra), which is the space between the eyebrows, for psychic vision and spiritual work, and it is beneficial when used for meditation or trance. In recent years it has been used to help others link to the alien vibration and all things extraterrestrial.

This is an attractive jasper crystal
that contains shades of olive green
and coral. Animal lovers gravitate
to unakite, as it links a person to
the animal kingdom and to nature.
If a pet goes missing, hold this
crystal in the hand and wish for
its return, as this is said to bring
good results. It also generates love
and compassion.

VANADINITE

Vanadinite is a reddish-brown crystal that is quite rare. It can be called an action stone, because it has a lively creative energy that helps get things done. This stone inspires journalists and authors to get rid of creative blocks, and if a person's libido is not good, this crystal is said to increase sexual stamina.

VITALITE

This is a pale, pinky-grey granite crystal
that has strong mentally restorative
powers, and it is used as a healing aid
for the vital organs. It is also good for at
dispelling negativity and anxiety, especially
within the workplace or when one is
in the public eye at conferences and
presentations. If someone feels bemused,
lost or fazed, vitalite can re-ground
the person.

WAVELLITE

Wavellite comes in many shades of green and yellow radial clusters, and it is quite rare. It is said to be useful when someone is dealing with cancer. An individual's intuitive vibration is heightened when owning this crystal because it helps to unlock buried knowledge and to enable the person to reach the higher self. This is a beautiful calming crystal that reminds a person who they really are.

WULFENITE

This stunning amber and orange mineral originated from Arizona, and although beautiful, there is a history of it being difficult to fashion into jewellery. It can help to banish sadness and bad habits that were learned in childhood, along with ridding the person of memories of trauma from previous lives. It acts as a mind and heart cleanser, enabling a person to move on to a freer life.

ZEBRA STONE

As the name indicates, this is a black-and-white striped crystal which is very attractive, and it also comes in a variety of other colours. It is a powerful healing crystal and is purported to help the pains of osteoporosis and other bone-related conditions. Stiff necks, joint pain and muscle spasm react well to this healing stone.

ZOISITE

A green and pink mineral that contains other colours and each one is unique. When the heart is saddened and depressed, this stone can be a useful pick-me-up, because it works quite quickly to dispel grief or sad memories. In ancient folklore, if a barren woman wore zoisite in her garments, it was said to aid fertility.

CHAPTER

3

ALL ABOUT CRYSTALS

This chapter will give you lots of useful information about crystals and their uses. Some of the ideas here cover practical matters, while others are spiritual in nature.

CRYSTALS

in groups

Crystals make perfect ornaments, but their energies may conflict, so it is best not to display them too close together. Leave enough room around each one so that it can give off its own personal energy. Dot crystals throughout the house and limit three or four to each room.

FINDING

and losing your stones

Crystals select their owners, so stones given to a person as a gift will often go missing or become lost, and certain gemstones tend to fall out of jewellery. If this happens to a person, they have to accept that it was not the right crystal for them. The same can be said for crystals that one might find on the ground, because if you find one, you should pick it up and keep it.

CRYSTALS

under the bed

This idea is becoming popular with crystal healers as the crystals connect with the seven chakras of the body. When a person is ill or run down, the person can place healing crystals in or under their bed at night to aid the healing process. This can cause nightmares, so the person should use protective stones, such as turquoise or tourmaline.

crystal
BLESSING

Every home should have at least one blessing every year, and those who practice this activity will use crystals to do this. Clear and smoky quartz tumble stones will be dotted around in each room and white tealight candles will be burned beside them. To rid a home of spirits, one would replace the quartz with black tourmaline or obsidian.

crystals for
BUSINESS

If a person is self-employed or if they own
a business, aventurine and carnelian work
well if kept in a cash register or situated
somewhere near coins or bank notes.
These crystals need to be cleansed at least
once a month to boost the good fortune.

crystals and
CHILDREN

Children are fascinated by crystals and some even want to start their own collection. If they are interested, the following stones will blend with a child's energy:

- Amethyst: a gentle lavender stone that brings love and healing
- Alexandrite: comes in various colours and gives self-esteem and confidence
- Olivine: a bright green stone for good luck

crystals for
CREATING

If there is a creative time up ahead, such as home décor, sewing, knitting or jewellery-making, placing certain crystals in the workplace can influence a person's creativity. Aventurine will calm and clear the mind for new ideas to filter through and for one's perception to be heightened.

crystals for
HEALING

There are numerous crystals one can use for the purpose of healing, so researching which stone is best for a specific ailment is a must. For general health issues, one might use blue lace agate, amazonite and amethyst as a starting point. Having the crystal in the home or carrying it in a pocket will help the healing process to begin.

crystals to heal
THE PAST

Desert rose is a beautiful, unusual crystal shaped like rose petals, and these formations are called gypsum. It channels new energetic movement and will clear out the baggage of the past, thus enabling a sense of wellbeing and acceptance over things that cannot be undone. This stone can also inspire the imagination, giving the wearer a clearer vision of the future.

crystals for the
IMAGINATION

Azurite is a stunning and rare blue crystal, and, if held in the hands for a few minutes, it is said to inspire the imagination for colour, texture and creativity. The deep green and flecked bloodstone will awaken the imagination for anything related to painting and writing.

crystals for a lost
ANIMAL

When a beloved animal strays, it's heartbreaking for the owner, and some say it's as bad as losing a child. If everything has been tried to retrieve it and there are still no answers, powerful crystals can be used. Place Dalmatian jasper on a photograph of the animal and ask for its return.

crystals
FOR LOVE

Each and every one of us wants perfect love and companionship and there are certain crystals to attract that energy:

- Rose quartz: a beautiful pale pink crystal with a pure vibration that attracts romance
- Opal: attracts love and passion
- Lapis lazuli: deep blue for friendship and harmony

crystals for
FOR LUCK

Crystals have been used as talismans for centuries, and many are said to bring good luck to the owner. Those who are superstitious and wish to attract luck carry stones such as amber, garnet and zircon. Place the lucky stones in a small pouch when attending job interviews or examinations, as these often empower the wearer.

crystals for
MEDITATING

There are many stones one can use to assist in a successful meditation. Selenite, amethyst and azurite are renowned for being some of the best for helping one to focus on the vibrational frequencies. A person would select their chosen stone and lay on the bed with the crystal resting on their stomach while they meditate.

crystals for
MONEY

Often, when money is tight, crystals can give the bank balance a boost. Citrine, sunstone and tiger's eye will work well to remove financial blockages and allow the flow of cash to reach the owner. Keep these stones on show in the house, somewhere near the entrance or on window sills.

crystals for
OPTIMISIM

Bustamite is very similar to rose quartz in its appearance and it is said to be a joyous crystal of optimism that will awaken the inner child. If held in the hand for a little while it will lift the soul and give the person a real sense of wellbeing and optimism.

crystals for
PRAYER

Whichever faith one chooses to follow, prayer or spiritual communication can be enhanced with the use of certain crystals. Angelite, catlinite and opal are commonly used, along with kyanite and blue topaz. Some people believe that holding one of the chosen stones while praying will carry messages to one's creator.

crystals for
PROTECTION

It is wise to know the best protecting stones. A crystal collector will always have black tourmaline at hand and it will be prized in their collection. It doesn't have to be large, because even the tiniest piece is powerful. You can wear a cabochon round the neck, though many people will place a piece hidden in their clothing for protection.

crystals for
PSYCHIC
visions

Calcite is a vivid orange crystal that is widely used as marble for figurines and kitchen worktops. It is known to awaken the higher consciousness to inspire originality and psychic gifts. Mediums who are good at painting portraits of spiritual guides for their clients are known to have this crystal nearby for inspirational channelling.

crystals for
REAL ESTATE

If a person is desperately trying to sell their home but isn't having any luck, planting small slivers of citrine in the ground outside of the home will help to remove any blocks the property might have. Always be sure to remove the crystals on moving day or the new owners will not stay.

crystals to
CONNECT
with
SPIRIT
GUIDES

Celestite is a delicate, soft blue crystal that is said to be blessed by the angels and guides. It enables a person to raise their vibration so that an otherworldly connection can be made. When channelling one's spirit guide, a person would first bathe with their stone in the tub and then go to bed and fall asleep holding it.

CHAPTER

4

CRYSTAL CHAKRA COLOURS

Many crystal specialists and healers will place different coloured crystals on each of the chakras or power points of the body for more impact when healing.

When conducting a deep meditation, the subject should try to focus their attention on each chakra in turn. In doing so, they will draw energy through the crystals and empower the body. Performing a controlled breathing exercise during meditation will open the chakras, allowing them to receive the crystal's power.

Spiritual people often use specific stones in rituals and incantations to alter the energies around them and to achieve their desires. When a person concentrates their intent on a gem while simultaneously performing an incantation, the power each crystal holds is thought to be enhanced.

ROOT CHAKRA

red jasper

The root chakra is located at the bottom of the spine and the genital area, and it deals with both physical movement and spiritual growth. It is also linked to the sexual muscles. When red jasper is placed on the root chakra area, it brings judgement when making decisions for relationships.

SACRAL
CHAKRA
carnelian

The sacral chakra is positioned in the lower abdomen and is linked to fertility, sex and relationships. It helps to make wise choices when going out into the world. The carnelian placed on the sacral chakra is linked with family life and healthy children.

SOLAR PLEXUS CHAKRA

citrine

The solar plexus is located in the abdomen and will boost self-confidence and personal growth to aid a person to their full potential. Citrine, when placed on this area, is a good chakra cleanser, imparting optimism and wealth. It acts similarly to an uplifting tonic.

HEART CHAKRA

rose quartz

The heart chakra, which is positioned in
the middle of the chest area, represents
deep feelings of love with a partner, family
members and friends. It can signify new love
and relationships too. By placing the rose
quartz on the heart chakra, it heightens the
vibrational frequency to a deeper love.

THROAT CHAKRA

blue calcite

Many blue crystals can be chosen for the throat chakra to help a person speak the truth and to bring confidence when making decisions through communication. Blue calcite is a soothing crystal, especially when angry emotions are involved; it tones down rash words, making a person more discreet.

THIRD EYE
CHAKRA
lapis lazuli

The third eye chakra, which is between the eyebrows, opens the consciousness to the unseen, the spiritual realms and self-expression. It can be an aid to psychoanalysing oneself deeply in the hope of improving the character. Lapis lazuli's crystal vibration is both rewarding and beneficial to mental health.

CROWN
CHAKRA
amethyst

This chakra is located at the crown of the head, and it is a powerful portal for inspirational energy that can motivate a person into a different way of thinking, and it is known as the umbilical cord that links man to the creator. The amethyst's pure energy is a powerful amplifier for the crown chakra.

CHAPTER

5

CRYSTALS
and
MAGIC

For any magic to be successful, one must first set up an area where the person intends to perform their crystal magic. This should be a quiet room in the house that is free of noise. Choose a suitable work surface to act as an altar, like a small table or a countertop.

the crystal
ALTAR

Items needed:

- A table or work surface
- A cloth of any colour (optional)
- The element of earth: a bowl of salt
- The element of air: sage or incense
- The element of fire: two white candles placed at either side of the table
- The element of water: a bowl of spring water or collected rainwater

the next steps

Once the altar has been set up, make sure that there are no disturbances, so turn off any devices that might be lying around and play some soothing tunes. There is a wealth of meditation or New Age music that can be downloaded from the internet.

Some people like to ring a little bell over the altar continuously for about a minute before any kind of crystal magic takes place. Use a small brass bell or even some Tibetan bells. Once finished, put the bell beside the other items on the altar, as this ensures that all the energies present are balanced and in tune.

CLEANSE
the STONE

Before the ritual starts, it is important to
prepare the crystal and cleanse it of any
residual energy it might have picked up. To do
this, see the section on crystal cleansing.

CALM the MIND

Before any ritual takes place, the spell-caster must be in the right frame of mind. If one has experienced a bad day or is feeling fraught, the connection to the crystals will not work as effectively. Also, wear loose-fitting clothing, so the energies pass through the person with ease.

FOCUS
on the INTENT

To bring about the desired results, light the two white candles and the incense, and sit in front of the altar. Holding the chosen crystal in the hands, the individual must concentrate for a few minutes on the problem they want to solve or objective they want to achieve, visualising the outcome they need in their mind's eye.

magical
NUMBERS

Practitioners often write their own mantras,
making sure that they're just a few lines long.
Words are always spoken from the heart and
then repeated seven, nine or twelve times.
Throughout time, these numbers have been
considered magical and, when vocalised
repeatedly, they create an energy that
connects with the universe.

TO END
the MANTRA

Once the mantra has been recited, always close the incantation with the words, "And now it is done." The crystals must then be placed onto the surface of the altar and left until the candles have burned for two hours. When the two hours are up, the mantra is complete and one can blow out the candles.

AFTER the MANTRA

When the rite is concluded, unless otherwise stated, the spell-caster must have the crystal with them for at least a week by keeping it in a pocket. This helps the person to absorb the power of the crystal and to achieve the desired results.

when
SLEEPING

Keeping the crystal close by when an individual is sleeping will also enhance the magic. If a small stone is used, the individual might like to place it inside their pillowcase, but resting it on a nightstand will work just as well. The crystal should always be in the vicinity of the practitioner.

TIME SCALE

If the crystal mantra is successful, the changed results should last for at least three months. Sometimes, it is necessary to repeat an incantation every so often to be sure that the power of the stone is continually charged up. Before any top-up magic takes place, one must make sure that the crystals are cleansed and blessed.

to cleanse and

EMPOWER

the altar

Clear quartz amplifies the power of every crystal nearby, so this ritual needs to be cast before any magical work takes place.

crystal

CLEAR QUARTZ

mantra

Repeat seven times

"I summon the
power, this magical
hour filled with grace,
I cleanse this space."

Place the quartz crystal in the centre of the
altar and leave it there during all rituals.

crystal

BLACK OBSIDIAN

mantra

Repeat twelve times

"My problems will vanish,
my troubles will flee.
My difficulties I banish,
and I will be free."

For one week, the crystal should be kept nearby
during the day and by the bedside at night.

to banish
BAD LUCK

For when life is one
long drama and a
person wants to bring
about peace.

for better

COMMUNI-CATION

When one needs
to bring about better
communications
between people.

crystal

Two pieces of

TIGER'S EYE

– holding one stone in each of the hands.

mantra

Repeat seven times

"We talk with ease; our issues will cease."

One crystal must be kept by the practitioner and the other must be given to the person with whom they want to communicate.

crystal

ORANGE CALCITE or CITRINE

mantra

Repeat nine times

"With this stone, my power I own, fearless and strong, all day long."

Place the crystal in the bowl of salt on the altar. Add a few grains of the altar salt to your cooking in the coming week.

to boost
CONFIDENCE

For whenever one needs to increase confidence or self-esteem.

to develop
CREATIVITY

For writers, musicians
and artists who want
to boost their talents.

crystal
JASPER

Put some of your work on the altar,
with a photograph of yourself.

mantra

Repeat seven times

"Unconfined, inspire my mind, my soul enthused with a crystal muse."

Make sure the jasper is always present in the
place where you are most likely to be creative.

crystal

MOLDAVITE

mantra

Repeat twelve times

"Hidden truths, let me see, with an open mind, it shall be. Nothing impedes, nothing restricts, with an unseen force, I shall predict."

It's important to wear the moldavite every time any kind of divination takes place.

to enhance

DIVINATION

For Tarot readers, palmists and psychics.

to control
EMOTIONS

When a person
needs restraint or
self-control.

crystal

LAZULITE

mantra

Repeat seven times

"Control my mind, at peace it shall be, limit my feelings, and set them free."

At times when one needs to contain emotions, ladies must place the stone inside their bra and men must carry it in a pocket.

crystal
FLUORITE

Wear this as jewellery, but a stone will suffice.

mantra

Repeat nine times

"Create a forcefield all around, negative vibes I will rebound."

The individual must be sure to carry or wear this stone to repel any negative energy from invading the person's space.

to guard against

NEGATIVE PEOPLE

For those who are around negative people on a regular basis.

a

FERTILITY

ritual

For women who have
trouble conceiving.

crystal
AVENTURINE

Lay this on a bed of fresh basil in a bowl
and place it on the altar.

mantra

Repeat twelve times

"A cherished child,
I yearn to receive,
a blessed baby is
my need."

Take the bowl and stone to the bedroom and
make love every night under a full moon.

crystal

MAGNETITE

mantra

Repeat twelve times

"Take this sorrow,
bury it deep, replace
with joy that
I can keep."

Make sure the stone is at least one mile from
the house and bury it in the ground.

to replace sadness
with

HAPPINESS

To remove all sadness
from life and bring
about happier times.

to turn a

NEGATIVE

into a

POSITIVE

For times in life
when all is hopeless
and a positive
outcome is needed.

crystal

PINK HALITE

mantra

Repeat nine times

"Things that have
hindered, and things
that have harmed, are
replaced with positive
crystals charmed."

Take the halite and leave it somewhere
by the entrance to your home.

crystal

CARNELIAN

Place a photo of the sufferer on the altar
and lay the crystal on top.

mantra

Repeat seven times on a
new moon phase.

"Illness be gone, there shall be none. Healthy and free, so mote it be."

Keep the crystal in the bedroom to work
throughout the night.

a general

HEALING MANTRA

For those that suffer
poor health.

bring

RELIEF

from

COLDS

and # FLU

Works especially well
when a cold will not
clear up.

crystal

RED JASPER

Light a eucalyptus incense stick.

mantra

Repeat seven times

"Magic unfold
and cure this cold,
allow me to breathe,
soothe and ease."

Carry the crystal around for the next few days
and the symptoms should fade away.

crystal

GREEN TOURMALINE

mantra

Repeat twelve times

"Bring healing for [name] renewed and restored, onwards and upwards and moving forth."

Give the crystal to the sufferer and tell them to keep it close by.

to heal after
SURGERY

This speeds up the healing process for anyone recovering after surgery, and it is best done on a waning moon. It is always better to do this for someone else rather than for oneself.

for those who
want to

LOSE
WEIGHT

crystal
APATITE

Set up the altar in the kitchen or on a worktop.

mantra

Repeat three times

"Slim I shall be, cravings shall end with the powerful magic this crystal sends."

Keep the crystal in the fridge and bring it out when you are preparing food or when tempted to grab a snack.

crystal

HEMATITE

On the evening of a waning moon, sprinkle
the crystal with cayenne pepper.

mantra

Repeat nine times

"Determination I shall find, all failures I shall leave behind."

It's important to carry or wear this crystal
for the next few weeks.

to increase
WILLPOWER

For anyone wanting
to break the habit of
drugs and alcohol.

to boost

FINANCES

When money is tight
and you need a little
extra to pay the bills.

crystal

SUNSTONE

Put the crystal on the altar underneath
a bank note.

mantra

Repeat nine times

"Hardship I face, let prosperity
flow, very soon my purse will
grow. Abundance and riches
come unto me, with the power
of magic, so mote it be."

Leave the crystal on a south-facing window sill.

crystal

Four small

CITRINE

tumble stones – smear the stones with
a little bergamot oil.

mantra

Repeat nine times

"My work life is great, this is my fate, a new job soon, by the power of the moon."

Place the stones in each corner of your bedroom.

to get a
NEW JOB

For all those who are seeking employment, perform this ritual on a new moon.

to
SUCCEED
in EXAMS

Good for those who are taking exams or a driving test.

crystal

AMBER

mantra

Repeat seven times

"I will succeed and I will thrive, my mind will be in overdrive."

Put the stone in an envelope and post it back
to yourself, then carry it when taking tests.

crystal

AMETHYST

mantra

Repeat twelve times during
the ritual and again before sleep

"When the day turns dark
and time for sleep,
this crystal stone, I shall keep.
Sleepy slumber, dreaming well,
a restful night with this spell."

Sleep with the crystal under the pillow.

to combat
INSOMNIA

When sleep just
won't come.

to find

TRUE LOVE

For those
looking for love.

crystal

ROSE QUARTZ

Burn an additional pink candle on the altar
on a full moon phase.

mantra

Repeat nine times

"New love I seek and
I shall find, a person who
is caring loving and kind.
I send my message for those
to hear, bring my
beloved partner here."

Carry the stone when out and about.

crystal

ALEXANDRITE

mantra

Repeat twelve times

"Time to leave,
this I know,
with strength of mind,
I shall go."

Take the crystal to a crossroads and leave it on
the ground before walking away.

to find

STRENGTH

to end a
relationship

For people who are
unhappy but lack the
courage to leave an
unhappy relationship.

CHAPTER
6

CRYSTALS
and
NATURE

crystals and
HOUSE
PLANTS

Just as we can respond to the power of a crystal, so can plants and flowers. If you have a house plant that is sulking, push a small piece of moss agate into the soil of the pot to stop it from feeling sorry for itself and encourage it to grow.

crystals in the
GARDEN

Placing crystals all around the garden will make everything prosper. Malachite adores any flowers with pink and purple hues, so just rest one near the base of the plant to ensure its happiness. For other flowers, one might choose green calcite, clear quartz or perhaps a small piece of tiger's eye.

crystals and
CROPS

Keen gardeners are not averse to trying a little crystal therapy to help their crops flourish and thrive. When planting vegetables in the ground or in raised beds, one might mix together a few handfuls of moonstone and citrine chips before digging them into the soil.

crystals and
TREES

Trees are particularly sensitive to the crystal energy and love nothing more than to grow alongside a buried gemstone. When planting trees, dig a large enough hole, making sure there is plenty of room for the roots, and place a piece of malachite or tree agate in the ground before introducing the tree to the soil.

crystals and
WILDLIFE

Garden visitors like birds, ants, hedgehogs
and bees all get a feel-good factor when
gemstones are near. Try hanging a crystal
pendulum from your bird table and watch
how the wildlife reacts. Nestling a few
pieces of quartz around a garden pond
will bring a tranquil energy to the
pond-life.

crystals and
NATURE
SPIRITS

If you believe in fairies and nature spirits, create a circle of pretty crystals somewhere in your garden. This is called a fairy ring and is thought to bring luck to the household. Dryads, tree spirits and even small pixies have been seen by some people who have the ability to psychically tap into adjacent realms.

CHAPTER
7

CRYSTALS

for

AILMENTS

This information might bring relief from even
the harshest of illnesses.

Just believe in the power of the crystal and make sure to follow the cleansing and preparation procedures mentioned earlier in this book.

After cleansing the crystal, one should rest on the bed with some soft music playing in the background. The lights should be turned down low. Rest the chosen crystal in the left hand (nearest the heart) and let it remain there for a minimum of thirty minutes. Repeat this every day until the person feels better.

for
AUTISM

Many people on the autistic spectrum have an affinity with crystals and some believe that they are sensitive to the energies they transmit. If an autistic person is distressed or anxious, deal with them and then hold a piece of sodalite in each hand or place it somewhere in the bedroom where the autistic person sleeps, as this will transmit a calming effect.

for
BACKACHE

If it is possible to lie on one's stomach, place a reasonably sized piece of howlite directly on the painful area. If not, place it on the bed and rest one's back on the stone. This crystal has the ability to draw out the pain, relaxing the muscles and relieving discomfort.

for
CYSTITIS

To help settle and heal an infection or to keep cystitis at bay once it has cleared up, the healing properties of danburite are believed to bring effective results. For treating any other bladder ailments, additional stones that can help are angel aura quartz and moonstone.

for
EARACHE

If a person is suffering from an ear infection or just simply pain in the ear, agate and onyx are great naturopaths. For this healing session, one would need two pieces of either stone to rest by each of the ears. Even if only one ear is affected, it is important to use two to balance the energies. Rest with the stones for thirty minutes a day. In folklore, a piece of onion in the ear is said to help.

for
HEAD ACHES

Lapis lazuli heals and comforts sore heads. A person must rest the stone near to where the pain is and hold it there for as long as possible. If the headache is more severe, amethyst and rose quartz are wonderful soothers.

for
HEART
PROBLEMS

Kunzite and jade are believed to prevent heart attacks and help with anxiety or any kind of heart defect. Place the stone directly over the heart, and after around fifteen minutes, the person might begin to feel a healing sensation emanating from the crystal. Repeat this exercise once a day.

for
JOINT PAIN

For those who suffer from one of the
many forms of joint pain, aquamarine,
black tourmaline and amethyst can bring
relief. Having one of the crystals nearby
at all times is necessary, so it is a good
idea to wear the stone as jewellery.

for
SINUSES

If an individual should suffer with sinus infections, allergies or even more extreme conditions such as rhinitis, the healing properties of fluorite and emerald will certainly help. Choose a stone and hold it close to the nose for as long as possible. Sometimes, resting it on the forehead has the same effect.

for
STOMACH
PAIN

For stomach ulcers, rhodonite placed
on the lower abdomen can bring relief.
For bloating, IBS and constipation, one
might choose aquamarine or carnelian.
For nausea, try black obsidian and rose
quartz, and for other gastric problems,
malachite and emeralds are favourable.

for
SKIN conditions

Jade, turquoise and amethyst possess restorative properties that can help to clear up most skin conditions. Make a crystal elixir by submerging one of the stones in a bowl of water for one minute and then dabbing the water onto the skin with a cotton wool pad. Repeat this daily for best results.

CONCLUSION

Crystals are addictive, and once you start to collect them and acquire an assortment, there is always a new one that will turn up when you're least expecting it and you'll be compelled to buy it. These precious and semi-precious stones hold a power like no other, and once you begin to tune into their vibration and understand their magic, they will reward you by enriching your life in so many ways.

INDEX

agate 24, 27, 170, 173, 182
agate (blue lace) 87
agate (moss) 170
agate (tree) 173
alexandrite 85, 166
amazonite 87
amber 92, 161
amblygonite 26
amethyst 25, 85, 87, 93, 111, 162, 183, 185, 188
angelite 96
apatite 153
aquamarine 185, 187
aventurine 84, 86, 141
azurite 89, 93

barim (barite) 27
beryl 28
bloodstone 89
bustamite 95

cacoxenite 29
calcite 98, 130
calcite (blue) 109
calcite (green) 171

carnelian 31, 84, 106, 146, 187
cassiterite 30
catlinite 96
celestite 101
citrine 32, 94, 99, 107, 130, 158, 172

danburite 181
datolite 33
desert rose 88
diamond 6, 7, 34

emerald 35, 186, 187
erythrite (cobalt boom) 36

fluorite 37, 138, 186
fuchsite 38

gabbro 39
garnet 92
goldstone 40
graphite 7
halite (pink) 145
hematite 41, 154

hemimorphite 42
howlite 180

iolite 43
ironstone 44

jade 45, 59, 184, 188
jasper 46, 71, 133
jasper (Dalmatian) 90

kinoite 47
kunzite 48, 184
kyanite 96

labradorite 49
lapis lazuli 91, 110, 183,
lazulite 50, 137

magnetite 142
malachite 51, 171, 173, 187
moldavite 52, 134
moonstone 53, 172, 181

natrolite 54
nuummite 55

obsidian 56, 83, 126, 187
olivine 85
onyx 182
opal 57, 91, 96

peridot 58
prehnite 59

quartz (angel aura) 181
quartz (clear) 60, 83, 124–5, 171, 174
quartz (faden) 61

red jasper 105, 149
rhodonite 187
rhyolite 62
rose quartz 63, 91, 95, 108, 165, 183, 187
ruby 64

selenite 65, 93
sodalite 66, 179
sunstone 94, 157

tanzanite 67

tiger's eye 68, 94, 129, 171
topaz (blue) 96
tourmaline 82
tourmaline (black) 83, 97, 185
tourmaline (green) 150
turquoise 69, 82, 188

ulexite 70
unakite 71

vanadinite 72
vitalite 73

wavellite 74
wulfenite 75

zebra stone 76
zircon 6, 92
zoisite 77